I Can Make a Difference

Helping in the Community

Vic Parker

www.raintreepublishers.co.uk

Visit our website to find out more information about Raintree books.

To order:

☎ Phone 0845 6044371
▤ Fax +44 (0) 1865 312263
▣ Email myorders@raintreepublishers.co.uk

Customers from outside the UK please telephone +44 1865 312262

Raintree is an imprint of Capstone Global Library Limited, a company incorporated in England and Wales having its registered office at 7 Pilgrim Street, London, EC4V 6LB – Registered company number: 6695582

Edited by Daniel Nunn, Rebecca Rissman, and Sian Smith
Designed by Steve Mead
Picture research by Ruth Blair
Production by Eirian Griffiths
Originated by Capstone Global Library Ltd
Printed and bound in China by South China Printing Company Ltd

ISBN 978 1 406 23441 1
16 15 14 13 12 11
10 9 8 7 6 5 4 3 2 1

British Library Cataloguing in Publication Data
Parker, Victoria.
  Helping in the community. -- (I can make a difference)
  1. Voluntarism--Juvenile literature. 2. Community life--Juvenile literature.
  I. Title II. Series
  302.1'4-dc22

Acknowledgements
We would like to thank the following for permission to reproduce photographs: Corbis pp. 7 (© Tim Pannell), 8 (© Ariel Skelley/Blend Images), 10 (© Ian Lishman/Juice Images), 22 (© Mika), 23 (RelaXimages), 24 (© Philippe Lissac /Godong), 29 (© Tim Pannell); Getty Images pp. 4 (Colin Hawkins), 6 (Justin Sullivan), 11, 17 (Jupiterimages), 12 (Gage), 13 (Stuart Fox), 18 (Design Pics/SW Productions), 19 (Ryan McVay); iStockphoto pp. 14 (© Andreas Reh), 20 (© Steve Debenport), 25 (© Grady Reese); Shutterstock pp. 9 (© Goodluz), 15 (© wavebreakmedia ltd), 16 (© Terrie L. Zeller), 21 (© Anette Linnea Rasmussen), 26 (© Lucky Business), 27 (© auremar).

Cover photo of a child with shopping reproduced with permission of Photolibrary (Randy Faris/Corbis).

Every effort has been made to contact copyright holders of material reproduced in this book. Any omissions will be rectified in subsequent printings if notice is given to the publisher.

Contents

Some words are shown in bold, **like this**. You can find out what they mean by looking in the glossary.

Why help?

Volunteering means spending your time and energy being helpful. Many people, places, and animals need all sorts of help. By helping, we can make the world a better, happier place.

Anyone can volunteer to help, young or old.

Knowing that you have been helpful can make you feel really good.

Volunteering can also give you the chance to:

- try new things

- go to new places

- make new friends

- increase your skills

- have fun!

 Before you help anyone, always get permission from a parent or guardian.

How can I help in my community?

Your **community** can be the people and area in which you live. It can also be other groups of people you meet with and areas you go to, such as your school or your **cultural community**.

Your community may have its own language, traditions, and celebrations.

You can help the other members of your community by thinking of ways to be caring. You could help solve problems they have by **volunteering** to help, getting other people involved, or by raising money, too.

Everyone in the world is part of one big community – the human race!

Helping new people in the community

It can be difficult for someone new to a **community** to make friends and settle in. You can **volunteer** help by saying hello and making them feel welcome. But you must always check with your parent or guardian before you speak to a stranger.

Going to visit people who are new to a community can make them feel welcome.

Ask a parent or older brother or sister to help you bake a cake as a welcome gift for a new neighbour.

If there is a new member of a group you belong to, such as Rainbows or Beavers, you can help them by introducing yourself and your friends, and including them in your activities.

Helping your classroom community

There are lots of ways you can **volunteer** in your classroom. You can show you respect your teacher by offering to help with small tasks like giving out or collecting up books.

Helping your teacher can make their day easier and happier.

Working as a team is important in volunteering.

You can show you care for your classmates by looking out for anyone who is left out or not sure of what to do. Volunteering to pair up with someone can be a great help.

Helping your school community

Volunteering to help at your school can make it a better place for everyone to be. You could look for little ways to help, such as collecting paper for **recycling**. If your school has a garden, you could help by volunteering to work in it.

You could volunteer to help grow flowers and vegetables at school.

You can show others that you are responsible by volunteering.

You could also help in other ways, such as helping at a cake sale or at your school fete. These are great ways to raise money for your school.

Helping elderly people in the community

You might know an **elderly** person in your **community** who is often on their own and feels lonely. You could ask a grown-up if you could **volunteer** to visit them regularly to cheer them up.

Sometimes you can help other people just by spending time with them.

Ask a grown-up if you can volunteer to visit a retirement home, too. You could get a group of your friends to go along to entertain the residents by singing or dancing.

You can do things you enjoy to make other people happy.

Helping at a hospital

People who are patients in hospital often feel poorly and fed up. You could help by **volunteering** to make 'get well soon' cards. Getting a card brightens someone's day.

A nurse can hand out your cards to the patients.

Do you have any toys, games, or books that you no longer need? You could give them to a children's ward for the young patients to enjoy. This kind of help is called **donating**.

Make sure that the things you donate are in good condition.

Helping the homeless

Most **communities** have organizations that help **homeless** people. They offer food, clothes, and sometimes somewhere to sleep, too. You could **volunteer** to help by making food or **donating** old clothes and toys.

Children can be homeless as well as grown-ups.

If you tell your friends at school about homeless people, they might want to volunteer too.

You could also make up a story or a play about what it is like to be homeless to show your family, friends, or class at school. By spreading the word you can get other people to volunteer to help as well.

Helping people who help us

There are many people who give special help to our **community** through their jobs, such as fire fighters, police officers, and ambulance **paramedics**. You can help them by acting responsibly and staying safe, to make their jobs easier.

You can help by making sensible choices, such as crossing the road in the right place.

You must only dial 999 if it is a real emergency, and there are no grown-ups around to ask for help.

Sometimes, someone in your community might need urgent help from a fire fighter, police officer, or ambulance crew. You can help both them and the emergency services by dialling 999 and answering the **operator's** questions clearly and calmly.

Thinking small

Sometimes little things can help in big ways. For instance, when you are in a library looking through books, give them to a librarian to put back on the shelves in the right place, so others can find them easily.

When you need to talk in a library, it also helps other people if you talk quietly.

You can help others by waiting your turn.

Volunteering to help in a **community** can sometimes mean choosing *not* to do things, too. For example, at school it is helpful *not* to run or push past people, but to be patient and let others go first.

Thinking big

You might want to raise money for an expensive **community** issue, such as a scheme that helps sick children's dreams come true. For this, you will need to get lots of other people to help you.

If you belong to a group such as the Scouts, you could find other **volunteers** there too.

A sponsored readathon is a great way to raise money.

In a group, you can raise money by asking people to **donate** things for a table-top sale. Or you could do a **sponsored** event, where people promise to give you money for completing a challenge, such as swimming several lengths of a pool.

Thinking even bigger

You might want to help very large **communities** with big problems. For example, helping people in another country who are starving. You could raise money by saving your pocket money for a month and **donating** it to a **charity**.

If you don't get pocket money, you could ask your parents if you could do jobs around the house to earn some money instead.

Telling others about a problem can be an important way to **volunteer** help.

You could make badges and posters about the issue, to spread the word and encourage others to help, too. You could also ask a grown-up to help you to write a letter or e-mail to the **politicians** who run countries to see if they can help.

Volunteer checklist

To be a good **volunteer**, you need to:

- be friendly

- suggest ideas but listen to others, too

- share and take turns, if you are in a team

- keep your promises

- treat other people the way you would like to be treated

- be keen and have lots of energy.

Most importantly, *always* check with your parent or guardian before you volunteer to help outside your home. Then they can make sure that you will be safe. They may even want to help!

Working with other people you know well can be a safe way to volunteer.

Glossary

charity organization that helps others

community group of people who live, work, play, or do other things together

cultural community group of people who originally came from the same area. They may have things in common, such as the languages they can speak.

donate to give away something that is of use to someone else

elderly old

homeless without a place to live. Many homeless people end up sleeping on the streets.

operator if you dial 999 in an emergency, the person who answers the phone to you is called the operator

paramedics ambulance drivers and crew who are specially trained to give medical help in emergencies

politicians the people who are in charge of running countries

recycling breaking down materials and using them again to make new things

sponsor to pay money to someone for completing a challenge. The money is then used to help someone or something.

volunteer offer to do something. Someone who offers to do something is called a volunteer.

Find out more

Books

Good Relationships (Exploring Citizenship), Vic Parker (Raintree, 2010)

Improving Our School Grounds (Start-Up Citizenship), Louise and Richard Spilsbury (Evans Brothers, 2007)

Teach Your Granny to Text and Other Ways to Change the World (We Are What We Do), Community Interest Company (Walker, 2008)

Communities (Investigate), Neil Morris (Raintree, 2010)

Websites

kidshealth.org/kid/feeling/thought/volunteering.html
Find out about how families can volunteer.

pbskids.org/itsmylife/emotions/volunteering
This website will help you think about how you could begin volunteering.

www.do-it.org.uk/
This website has the details of thousands of organizations that need volunteers.

Index